# The Encl

## Reflections on The Way of the Cross

Vincent Sherlock

*VERITAS*

First published 1999 by
Veritas Publications
7/8 Lower Abbey Street
Dublin 1

Copyright © Vincent Sherlock 1999

ISBN 1 85390 447 3

Reprinted 2005

Design by Bill Bolger
Photographs by Valerie O'Sullivan
Printed in Ireland by Betaprint Ltd, Dublin

# Introduction

The Stations of the Cross are fourteen windows through which we catch glimpses of the sufferings of Christ. More than that, however, they call us to see beyond the obvious and to find the present-day faces that reflect this suffering. They are at their best when they urge us to respond with Veronica of the sixth station, the women of the eighth and the good thief who is to be found somewhere in the eleventh.

In the pages that follow, we will meet the face of Christ in the face of a teenager, an alcoholic, a young student, an elderly woman and many others.

In praying these pages, it might be helpful to see our place in this Way of The Cross not so much as that of onlooker but rather of one being invited to meet the Lord in the everyday situations and people that surround us.

'Insofar as you did it for one of the least of these, you did it for me' (Mt 25)

*I saw the dangers and yet I passed*
*along the enchanted way,*
*and I said let grief be a fallen leaf*
*at the dawning of the day*

Patrick Kavanagh

A young African gathers some food and a few bottles of water. He heads for the docks, having heard of a ship's departure for Europe. He has been told it will stop off in Ireland. He hides himself in the bowels of the ship. The cargo is his only companion. He did not realise the power of the fumes. In Cork, his body is discovered beside his still unopened food and drink...

# I

## The First Station
### Jesus is condemned to death

We adore you, O Christ, and praise you – because, by your Holy Cross, you have redeemed the world.

Dear Lord, help us to realise that we must see this young man's face at the First Station. If we fail to do this and take real notice of our brothers and sisters of every nationality and creed, the violent deaths will continue – from the pain of suicide to the tragedy of accidents – from the African stowaway to the elderly neighbour.

*O that we would listen to his voice, let us harden not our hearts.*

She is fifteen, he soon becomes her first love. No day passes without a meeting or a phone call. Time passes so quickly in his company. His love is professed as often as they meet. The relationship moves on a few months but their experimentation a few years – 'I think I'm pregnant', she confides in the darkness. The darkness does not disguise his shock and, as his arm pulls away from her she realises, that though she shares equally the responsibility for what has happened she'll have to face it alone....

# II

## The Second Station
### Jesus is made to carry his cross

We adore you, O Christ, and praise you – because, by your Holy Cross, you
have redeemed the world.

Dear Lord, if we do not see her in this second station, it's little more than a
piece of plaster on our walls. It calls out to us – have a heart for those in crisis.
You found your strength in family and friends. We pray that all who are
heavily laden may not be found in need of support.

*O that today we would listen to his voice, let us harden not our hearts.*

It's 3 o'clock on a Saturday morning. The hours have passed quickly. 'Be home by 2.00 a.m.', his mother calls as he heads for the bus that suggested he'd travel in safety. The music pounds and the lights bring out colours and moods in his friends he had never noticed before. 'Try one of these', one of them shouts over the noise as he holds a tablet between his fingers. It will do no harm, he is assured, but be sure to drink plenty of water afterwards. 'Be home by 2…' seems so far away now as his hand stretches to the supposed joy on offer…

# III

## The Third Station
### Jesus falls for the first time

We adore you, O Christ, and praise you – because, by your Holy Cross you have redeemed the world.

Dear Lord, it's a short step between being upright and on the ground. It might be a push or a slip but the result is the same. With you, many are on the verge of that first fall. Give them strength to realise that there are other ways. Remind them that the road will always have its ups and downs but we must push on none the less. Deliver our young friend from this first fall and continue to encourage us to choose life for others and ourselves.

*O that today we would listen to his voice, let us harden not our hearts.*

He hasn't come home yet. She remembers the early days of marriage. He'd come home from work and the times they'd have together. Then the homecomings got delayed and the time alone increased. Often she remembers Neil Diamond's famous song, 'You don't bring me flowers any more'. The headlamps of his car light up the bedroom wall. Tense, she waits to determine his mood in the opening of the front door. It's an angry opening. She hears the dinner plate crash to the floor in the kitchen. The dinner had burned itself out on that plate four or five hours earlier. She braces herself as he bullies open the bedroom door. As she defends herself and tries to reason with him, she sees her young son at the bedroom door. She tries to pretend it's a game but as their eyes meet across an angry man, they know too well that the game is for real.

# IV

## The Fourth Station
### Jesus meets his mother

Dear Lord, there are meetings that you'd imagine should never take place. This fourth station is a difficult meeting. What thoughts go through your mind as you look across the angry gathering? There was reassurance in it, however. Words were not necessary. Here, we meet this station in the bedroom of an angry home. The child's look seeks, in its innocence, to kiss things better and the mother's look says I am still here for you. Lord, strengthen family life and values. Rid our homes of violence.

*O that today we would listen to his voice, let us harden not our hearts.*

On a dark night, we round a corner to see a car with flashing hazard lights. The lights of our car catch a glimpse of a man battling with a punctured wheel. It's late and there's risk involved in stopping. We begin to justify the as yet unmade decision to pass by. 'He's bound to have a spare.' 'If he wanted help he'd have asked.' 'It's not safe to stop.' The inclination to pass by is strong and justifiable.

# V

## The Fifth Station
### Simon helps Jesus to carry his cross

We adore you, O Christ, and praise you – because, by your Holy Cross you have redeemed the world.

Dear Lord, they say that Simon was not a willing helper either. Soldiers forced his assistance, not out of any concern for the Lord's suffering but rather to hasten the work in hand. We can only imagine the comfort his help must have brought the Lord. It seemed so little and yet it meant so much. May this Station teach us never to underestimate the difference our help can make.

*O that today we would listen to his voice, let us harden not our hearts.*

For years he has tried to hide it. Hours spent before his bedroom mirror, practising repeatedly his now standard answer to the teachers' questions. 'I don't know'. The teachers have stopped noticing, in fact they don't ask him questions anymore. What's the point – the answer will be the same: 'I don't know'. The sad thing, however, is that he does know. The answers are locked inside of him, the stammer with which he has been afflicted does not allow answers. Often in the night he recalls the taunts of fellow pupils – 'Wh… sha… whattttss… your … name?' A new teacher arrives – a question is asked – he freezes and then it happens, the girl in the desk behind him says 'Go on, you know the answer, don't be afraid'.

# VI

## The Sixth Station
### Veronica wipes the face of Jesus

We adore you, O Christ, and praise you – because, by your Holy Cross you have redeemed the world.

Dear Lord, help us to realise that Veronicas come in all shapes and sizes. She's a caring grandmother, a young nurse, a caring neighbour. For our friend, she's the one in the class who can see beyond the blemish and discover his hidden depths. More than that, she gives him the courage he thought he'd never find. She is the one who does the right thing since it is the right thing to do. Give us the heart and eyes of Veronica – that we may see beneath the surface.

*O that today we would listen to his voice, let us harden not our hearts.*

She has attended the weekly meetings. It took her a while to say 'My name is Joan and I am an alcoholic', but she remembers it clearly. 'Hello, Joan', was the response. There was no judgement involved. Indeed she had said hello to others as well but she never thought she'd have the courage to introduce herself. She's come a long way since that night. Her relationship with her husband and children has never been better but she hadn't bargained on today. There's a bottle in her hand, she bought it after her boss told her there'd have to be cutbacks in the office. Everything in her says 'Don't', but the seal has been broken and the trickle into a long unused glass becomes a flow.

# VII

## The Seventh Station
### Jesus falls the second time

We adore you, O Christ, and praise you – because, by your Holy Cross you have redeemed the world.

Dear Lord, if we don't see her on the ground with you, well may we weep. You have fallen for her. You gaze from your own awareness of being fallen and you see her through tear-filled eyes. You tell her that she can get up since there is more road to be travelled. People are depending on her as they are on you. You offer her strength to 'change the things she can'. Help us too, Lord, that we may see her need and encourage her to her feet.

*O that today we would listen to his voice, let us harden not our hearts.*

She often wonders where she went wrong. Others tell her that it's not her fault but it's poor consolation. She knows she tried her best but now she wonders was it enough. The reluctance had been there for a while. Each Sunday was a struggle. 'It's time for Mass', she'd call to him beneath a mountain of twisted bedclothes. 'In a minute', he'd answer. She remembers the first Sunday he said he wasn't going. Hints had been dropped for a while. He'd talk about boring sermons and an out-of-touch Church. It was the only Church she knew and she loved it. It's four years now since that Sunday and he has never gone since. What more could she have done… will he ever go back?

# VIII

## The Eighth Station
### Jesus meets the women of Jerusalem

We adore you, O Christ, and praise you – because, by your Holy Cross you have redeemed the world.

Dear Lord, it's hard to see people pull themselves away from you. It's especially hard for those who love them. In this Station you let us know that you notice the tears of those left to put the pieces together. You reassure the women that there's no need to cry for you but you tell them to cry for themselves. It's as if you're telling them they deserve to feel let down. Encourage us in our tears, help us not to lose courage. May those who have lost sight of you find you once again.

*O that today you would listen to his voice, let us harden not our hearts.*

Michael always feared it might end like this. No one realised the terrible pressure he suffered during his Leaving Cert year. It was a constant struggle. They were so proud when the Leaving results paved the way for a university scholarship. He will never forget the journey from his home to the university town. While it wasn't said, he knows that his father was recapturing missed opportunities from his own life. Now the noticeboard tells him he has failed – not for the first time – these were the repeats. He had tried to make little of the first set of results but there's no escaping this time. Maybe he should get away. He has a friend in London… or is it Manchester?

# IX

## The Ninth Station
### Jesus falls for the third time

Dear Lord, this Station demands that we feel the pain of this young man. There are some who would say he could have done better but only he himself knows the real truth of the situation. May he, and all who feel weighed down and worried, find strength in that great story you told … 'a certain man had two sons'. We pray for him and for all, that having come to their senses, they too may feel the father's embrace though they might yet be 'a long way off'.

*O that today you would listen to his voice, let us harden not our hearts.*

Whispers do their rounds; 'Did you hear what they're saying about him?' 'Go away out of that, I don't believe it'. 'Well, I don't know but they say it's fact'. The stories vary but there's consistency in the whispers. Someone needs taking down a peg and there's no better way to do it. It might be a person, or an institution or a business but the task in hand is to destroy by word of mouth and innuendo. There's great safety in 'they say', for no one is being involved. We like the anonymity it offers. 'Well I don't know, but they say'…

# X

## The Tenth Station
### Jesus is stripped of his garments

Dear Lord, help us to see the damage done to you in this Station. In its own way, it is among the cruellest of them for it was totally unnecessary. Who could have needed that garment? Would it ever be worn? Possibly it meant a lot to you but 'they' decided to take it none the less. Like the good name, it was all you had left but 'they' threw lots for it. The winning was unimportant, the stripping was all that mattered. Deliver us from all desire to belittle people by gossip and innuendo. There's so little to be gained and so much to be lost.

*O that today we would listen to his voice, let us harden not our hearts.*

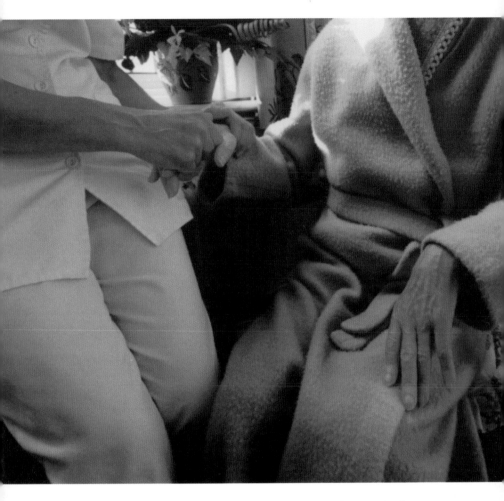

Mary sips slowly the cup of tea the young nurses' aide brought her at 4.15 p.m. She's sure of the time since that's the time for afternoon tea in St Angela's Nursing Home. It's like clockwork but then so is everything else. She knows it has to be this way. Mary smiles when she remembers the days she'd have a cup of tea whenever she felt like it. Those happy days when she could go and come as she pleased. 'Those were the days', she thinks to herself, 'and how I miss the freedom'. The time seems so long and she wonders will she ever get used to the idea of people having to do things that she once took for granted…

# XI

## The Eleventh Station
### Jesus is nailed to the Cross

We adore you, O Christ, and praise you – because, by your Holy Cross you have redeemed the world.

Dear Lord, help us to realise that you focus our minds on powerless limbs in this Station. You knew what it was to walk and to touch. Your legs had brought you many places and always with a purpose. Your hands had touched and blessed, fed and raised, healed and embraced. Now their power has been stolen. You call us to a deeper awareness of the Spirit and to realise that others have a responsibility to help.

*O that today we would listen to your voice, let us harden not our hearts.*

It wasn't altogether unexpected. He had been ill for some time. There was always a chance that he might make it but the doctors never held out much hope. It's sad just the same. He had a lot of life left in him and there was so much he wanted to give. Neighbours begin to gather in his home. It's strange without him in it – 'You'd almost expect to see him there in the corner' – but he's not there and he never will be again. May he rest in peace. So much will be said over the next few days. Things he did, places he went, friends he knew – they'll all be revisited in word, prayer and tears. Our hearts go out to those who are left behind. It will not be easy for them. In truth, we are 'sorry for their trouble' and God knows, we will miss him.

# XII

## The Twelfth Station
### Jesus dies on the Cross

Dear Lord, as we gaze at your lifeless body fill our hearts with memories of your word. Remind us of the places you have been, the things you have done and the people you have loved. As we look among their faces, may we find ourselves in the company of the Apostles, Lazarus, Martha, Mary, Jairus and his young daughter. As we recall your life, at the very moment of your death, may we know that you have always loved us.

*O that today we would listen to your voice, let us harden not our hearts.*

The years passed quickly. Their love, though not often mentioned, was more powerful now than at any moment in their past. She can't begin to imagine her days without him, though he had told her he'd soon be going. The doctor told her it would only be a matter of time and as the clock, a wedding present of forty-seven years ago, ticks towards 3.45 a.m. it seems to stop. The priest looks at her across the old wooden bed. Peter and herself often thought about getting a new one but it never seemed the right thing to do. Her children are with her and their children sleep in the beds of their parents … in Sean's room and Katie's room. 'He looks lovely, Mammy', whispers Katie and, as she looks at his closed eyes and silenced heart, she says 'Yes, Katie, he does'.

# XIII

### The Thirteenth Station
Jesus is taken down from the Cross

We adore you, O Christ, and praise you – because, by your Holy Cross you have redeemed the world.

Dear Lord, our traditions have taught us how to show respect to the dead. Conscious of the grief of others, we bless ourselves as even a stranger's coffin passes by. Help us always to show our respect for those left to grieve. This Station shows us a family in grief and reminds us that some of that grief must be shared by ourselves.

*O that today we would listen to his voice, let us harden not our hearts.*

As a family, they never gave that piece of ground much thought. They often thought that they'd not like to have it next door to their own home. It's the living we need to fear all right, but there's something eerie about a graveyard just the same. It was a place to go with a crowd at the time of a funeral and usually there'd be need for an umbrella. The closing decade would be answered from the edge of the crowd: 'Are you speaking to them?' 'No, I saw them last night'. Now it's a regular part of the weekly, and sometimes daily, routine. Thoughts are shared and tears are dropped alongside the 'Kneel and Pray' inscription in concrete. It's a year now, since their daughter was laid to rest.

# XIV

## The Fourteenth Station
## Jesus is laid in the tomb

We adore you, O Christ, and praise you – because, by your Holy Cross you have redeemed the world.

Dear Lord, in this station we pray for all who have died. We remember them on bended knee in the cemeteries of our land and in the quietness of our hearts. We pray that they may rest in the peace they sought in life, and that from their place of rest, they may guide, console and urge us onward as we continue the journey of life.

*O that today we would listen to his voice, let us harden not our hearts.*

To fulfil the scripture perfectly,
he said 'I am thirsty'.